I recently contacted a media
theorist and decided that my 1600 words
on Psychiatry's Messiah and the Celebrity
End of Times Plot isn't convincing enough
and to be quite frank as the so called
Messiah of all mankind I'm sick of being
tortured.

"In space no one can hear you scream"
and I also doubt that this reaches anyone
hence my moral ambiguity of how it will
affect anyone including myself.

The truth is the media is getting worse -
they present a monster and Michael Stype
from REM in his 1995 Slaine concert in his
Monster World tour, that I attended,
suggested it was not applicable in this
case.

I am sick of excusing torturers and telling everyone that up until psychiatry I was in the voluntary sector doing work for vulnerable people.

But as the Harry Potter Keeper of Secrets - as powerful as Lord Voldemorte himself - I decided to initiate change in my horrible existence.

The Story starts in Northern Ireland a country with 6 war torn counties and the Star of David as part of its flag. Born in 77 to house number 7 at the Whit time of year (Pentecost a time when the local Passionate Monastery holds an annual family day) Northern Ireland was in for a lucky strike - until now!

Named Damien as a suggestion from my devil worshipping aunt (living outside Northern Ireland but with frequent visits) my name was possibly a joke from the 76 Omen film until it became clear that my aunt got precisely that. She tortured a baby - me and as a spying device had been put in my ear (beamed to the security services) she realised her cult had been rumbled. The pre-Thatcher UK government of the time wasted no time in selling me to the media and thus became The Truman Show "the first child ever to be legally adopted by a corporation" skilfully represented as Orphan Annie and Daddy Warbucks in the 1982 musical film.

Annie became my nickname it representing Anakin Skywalker as well and David was my tortured split personality.

My first outing in the media came I believe with the Stiff Little Fingers song Alternative Ulster (a name for Northern Ireland) but for the wider world it was in the Diffrent Strokes theme tune "then along come two they've got nothing but the genes." The celebrities rebuilt my country from scratch - ever hear about the 1998 Good Friday Agreement or Crucifixion Agreement as I like to call it? 1998 was my first stay in psychiatry for 6 weeks. Under the "loose affiliation of millionaires and billionaires and baby" (Graceland by Paul Simon) my country enjoyed the best consumer capitalism had to offer as seen if you look at the YouTube videos of adverts for our Christmas shopping during the troubles. I enjoyed them as well and don't want to take any street from any skateboarding kid in the world but I've been through enough.

This song from Diffrent Strokes alludes to the Clear Gene(s) and the guy I call Herbie (5/3) tortured in psychiatry alone since 1963. He might have done 27 years before that and was finally released somewhere at the time of Lonnie Gordon's Happnin All Over Again in 1990. The red jump suit of the 6 Million Dollar Man springs to mind - a couple of days in an American prison perhaps [hunt for Luke Skywalker ends].

Brainwashing is murder and I am that OCD and currently tortured that I will have to do a rushed job on this extended edition in something that could become the pamphlet releasing the spells of the conspirators of mankind's destinies. Look at the bible - why in the book of Daniel was the king's countenance constantly changing - why was Pharoah's heart hardened - in the latter case I blame the ceremonies at Karnak being so traumatic that they caused an intentional split personality for Egypt's priests to control.

Why Messiah - that's a strong word ("it is you who say it"). Well there's the 7's (perfect number) the Holy Spirit (Pentecost) , my mother and father - Mary and Joseph - Virgo and Aries. Mary means longed for child - she wanted a girl.
_____ Young my grandmother (important second name [Adam Young from Good Omens or the emphasis in some Paul Simon and other artists lyrics amongst other things]). Her name meant Heart of the Ocean or pearl and she lived beside the sea [the Indian Ocean according to Paul Simon's Graceland's Myth of Finger Prints].

There is my Jesus brain - I missed hate and developed love in its absence - my brain finally stopping developing at 9 in 1986 ("my travelling companion is 9 years old [Graceland Paul Simon]). With Chernobyl also that year (the Wormwood of Revelations), Haley's Comet, the death of Satan (L. Ron Hubbard) and the Knights of Columbanis finally getting my brain stopped just before lust at the precise moment after a hypnotic assault when a rock was thrown into a river reminiscent of another scene in Revelations. There's Herbie's Jesus Christ Superstar as the other guy this happened to and for me De Dannan's Operator from How the West Was Won.

Paul Simon in the song Proof in his Rhythm of the Saints album sang, "faith is an island in the setting sun, proof is the bottom line for everyone" and in Born at the Right Time he uses boy and girl as the same person as does much of the media this man having a little girl's brain.

I'm a fair witness and in case you think it is only devil worshippers that torture - the Catholic Knights of Columbanis (Columbus in America) tried to keep my brain arrested by causing more damage just before hatred at anger - yes by torture - using both kids and their paedophile adherents.

There are curses that withdraw the approval of the biblical beasts (from Revelations) to buy, sell, receive or give services and generally go about your life untortured. I count 3 beasts Catholic knight gran mal, Scientology Fairgame (exactly the same) and psychiatric patient's gran mal. Before birth my family was Fairgamed, Gran Maled - why?- because hatred breeds such intolerance and jealousy and wants to destroy.

My brain became the Phantom Menace - the holy grail of brain scans - if undamaged it would prove retardation by trauma and free a lot of tortured vulnerable adults and (as you will see) every one else besides.

I mention all these films but the meaning for films is in the trailers and this is my Ready Player One battle cry in the "war for control of the future" - Amor Proximi! - meaning love of neighbour from a Doctor Frasier Crane (Craney being the name of some of my family's ancestors and that being their Motto).

The guy I was emailing was a writer and audible speaker of musical conspiracy theories - he had most of the music industry's secrets bar the Messiah code. He mentions things in the popular media today like covering of one eye. The covered eye according to me represents the part of the brain that a person uses - love or hate. Most gran mals (arrested development psychiatric patients) can wink with their right eye - mine is the left. In the Goonies one eyed Willie has his left eye covered.

As I stated previously it's not only devil worshipers who use torture. The Catholic Knights tried to torture a second arrested development out of me from 5-9 the second one happening at an altar boy trip in 1986 described previously. The reason - "The Phantom Menace" my skipped stage of development of my brain (my whole story is in Weird Al Yankovitch's version of

the Phantom Menace - The Saga Begins).
If they had succeeded when they first tried
to cause a second arrested development I
would have no control emotion no hate nor
love - just attachment, fear and anger.

The reason such developmentally
challenged people (who have developed
love) are even more cursed (check Love in
the First Degree) - psychiatry always tries
a "Last Crusade" for the brain scan:

"Love is required whenever he's hired
Comes just before the kill
No one can stop him
No hit man can match him
For his million dollar scam
One golden shot means another poor
victim
Has come to a glittering end
For a price he'll erase anyone.
The man with the golden gun."

All bond theme tunes are about exactly the same thing Bond-villain-esque-super-shrinks. Compare Love in the First Degree with A-ha's the Living Daylights.

Listen the songs - watch the trailers (the 80's is full of films like DARYL, The Golden Child, Conan, Baby Secret of Lost Legend, Willow, Flight of the Navigator) listen the albums eg. Now 97 and the songs and movies from early 1998 are mostly me. As I wrote in the email:

"I have had creative input into such things - that ET looking thing in Neverending story is ET, the Golden Compass was a toy created by me from my grandfather's old wrist watch, the Ocarina of Time was bought in Madrid if not how come Americans can understand ocarina and not philosopher from the Sorcerer's Stone. My old school is Hogwarts (corridors move as there was constant building work) I just assume that with all the teachers and all and me going through that til 27 and a half it was MY interpretation of it all. It's playing fields were on Gallows Hill "the cross is in the ball park" Paul Simon."

Why publicise it: well you have to look to REM's What's the Frequency Kenneth (a reference to one time Minister for Health and Chancellor of the Exchequer of the Thatcher governments knowing the radio frequency of the aural implant/spying device). This is normally linked to an assault on a journalist by a guy claiming all media was about him (a cover up) and it explains that they were creating proof and a person to which it points:

"I studied your cartoons, radio, music, tv, movies, magazines.
Richard said withdrawal in disgust is not the same as apathy."

The song goes on to mention "you wore a shirt of violent green" a reference to Northern Ireland.

It's sister song the Sidewinder Sleeps Tonight says:

"Baby, instant soup doesn't really grab me
Today I need something more sub- sub- sub- substantial
A can of beans or black-eyed peas
Some Nescafé and ice
A candy bar, a falling star, or a reading from Doctor Seuss."

It goes on to say that the split personality they created was a machine that only swallowed money and was "computer designed."

The person to be woke up is the Queen of England hence the "only joking" bit when the head of the Scientology movement says to "tell her she can kiss my ass". The Queen is represented in much media even before 1977 (which could point to Herbie (5/3)'s origins) and is often called Betty - Call Me Al or Betty Boo Doing the Do. The latter song's lyrics are in the first person pretending to be the Queen ("there's not another MC who can beat the Queen") and they clearly refer to Northern Irish people: "you wear that sash I know you despise me."

I'm not very internet savvy but Amazon makes desktop publishing easy.

What follows is one draft of: Pamphlet On Psychiatry's Messiah and the Celebrity End of Times Plot:

This is a conspiracy (but not a theory) of this and the last century and I dread to think how many power-brokers were plotting.

It takes a while to get the gist of it but it's a popular media truth about two guys being tortured by scientology and then psychiatry since at least 1963 to the present day fulfilling scientology's version of the book of revelations by picking a Messiah. If you check all the media references I cite you'll see I'm on to the celibacy's (that's like democracy or autocracy only the celebrities are in control) greatest conspiracy.

"these are the days of lasers in the jungle, lasers in the jungle somewhere, staccato signals of constant information - a loose affiliation of millionaires and billionaires and baby." Paul Simon Graceland 1986.

And here it is - it's actually a number of conspiracies that fit into one - a conspiracy merely being two or more people plotting in secret:

To really understand what scientology has against psychiatry you have to know who peoples psychiatry.

The vast majority of psychiatric inmates are people who have had a gran mal trauma arresting their development (usually caused by child abusers using hypnosis) before the age of 6.

Until relatively recently all people with developmental issues ended up being institutionalised until some doctor exposed what the psychiatrists were doing to his Downs Syndrome daughter which eventually liberated people with predetermined genetic learning disabilities from the clutches of psychiatrists

Unfortunately there has never been a diagnosis of gran mal arrested development and psychiatry labels any other symptoms these people (known as the gran mals) might show as their condition ignoring the fact that these people have learning disabilities - something a psychiatrist could diagnose in a fraction of a second through sight alone.

They are spotted at an early age by the forces of the health and social services and the Catholic Knights that influence healthcare throughout the world (Knights of Columbus in America) and are forced into psychiatry to provide aversion therapies to other people who end up in psychiatry eg people with real bi polar disorder or people with addictions.

The way they treat people is generally disliked - you only need think of Elvis; "they said you were high class that was just a lie. You ain't never caught a rabbit and you ain't no friend of mine." I assume heartbreak hotel is about time spent in rehab as well.

L. Ron Hubbard had a plan. He devised this plan from the section of Revelations of the devoured man child and the red dragon. It is contained in his short speech that I call the 1984 assault weapon speech which can be found on youtube. It basically goes something like this:

THEREFORE WE REALLY DO HAVE THE REMEDY BEFORE THE ASSAULT WEAPON IS PRODUCED. YOU EVER HEAR OF 1984 BY POOR OLD GEORGE ORWELL YES YES THAT'S WONDERFUL. THAT COULD BE THE PALEST IMAGINED SHADOW OF WHAT A WORLD WOULD BE LIKE UNDER THE RULE OF THE SECRET USE OF SCIENTOLOGY WITH NO REMEDY IN EXISTENCE. AND ITS ALRIGHT IN THIS OFFHAND AGE TO JUST BRUSH THINGS ASIDE - ITS OF NO IMPORTANCE NO IMPORTANCE. AND LETS NOT BE DRAMATIC THE WAY PEOPLE ARE BEING DRAMATIC ABOUT THE ATOM BOMB. IN FACT THE ATOM BOMB ISN'T AS SERIOUS AS THIS ITS JUST A MEST WEAPON. AND ITS ALRIGHT TO BE LIKE THE LITTLE BOY WHISTLING IN THE DARK THERES NO GHOSTS OR BOOGEY MEN EXIST. WELL THIS BOOGEY MAN DOES EXIST. AND THERES A VERY SIMPLE REMEDY JUST MAKE SURE THAT THE REMEDY IS

PASSED ALONG. DON'T HOLD IT, DON'T HOARD IT AND IF YOU EVER DO USE ANY BLACK DIANETICS USE IT ALL ON THE GUY WHO PULLED SCIENTOLOGY OUT OF SIGHT SO THAT IT WASN'T AVAILABLE ANY MORE CAUSE HE'S THE BOY WHO WOULD BE ELECTING HIMSELF "THE NEW ORDER". WE DON'T NEED ANY NEW ORDERS ALL THOSE ORDERS AS FAR AS I'M CONCERNED HAVE BEEN FILLED.

After that someone gasps because L. Hubbard has predicted the second coming and apparently the order of satan and the anti-Christ (False Prophet) have already been filled.

So what does this mean on the ground?

Well you have to know something about brain development. After the initial attachment stages its Yoda from Star Wars. Fear leads to anger anger leads to hate. You can almost pin point the years of this development if you've seen a terrible twos tantrum - that look looks like hate but in fact it's pure rage - hate develops afterwards and calms the child down as hate is one emotion that controls both fear and anger. At about 5 or 6 another part of the brain begins to develop - love for about 4 years after which come lust, teenage angst and the brain slowly stops developing in the early 20's.

Well the gran mals gang trapped in psychiatry have no brain development in the love part of the brain - they had a trauma about 5 and they refuse to accept anyone with development in the love part of the brain. When L. Ron talks about the assault weapon being produced he is predicting a boy who has a gran mal trauma after 5 years of age and develops love. After being chased out of society and psychiatry the scientologists as ordered would use all their black dianetics and cause psychiatric conditions and body and brain damage so severe that the weapon would have to be admitted to a psychiatric hospital.

Thats where neurosurgeons come in. With their brain drugs and as Paul Simon calls it "Staccato signals of constant information." And attempt to reverse all damage done to the brain which wipes some of the memories of the brain also.

It seems that no doctor is willing to admit that non-genetic arrested development exists and prefer to label it as another condition. Gran mals have developmental issues which mimic the genetic learning disabilities brain but someone with full development up to 5 and then a few years more would somehow prove the existence of non-genetic gran mal trauma if they could just find someone who hasn't got any other conditions.

Heres where the celebrities come in - they sing they dance they make movies like Star Wars, the Golden Child, DARYL, the Last Star Fighter even the Omen, The life Of Brian and Jesus Christ Superstar and the theme tune to The Man With The Golden Gun by Lulu. ["Love is required whenever he's hired comes just before the kill"] why?

The Assault Weapon the Devoured Man-child from Revelations was thought to have been found as early as 1963. He had the mental age of an 8 year old. He had 5 years of development in the hate part of the brain and 3 years development in the love part of the brain - Herbie The Lovebug's number 5/3. He seems to have been involved with either scientology or psychiatry up until the 90's with Lonnie Gordon's Happnin All Over Again."And you're probably just tired of hearing it all the time on every song every lyric and every rhyme "(Eminem) the popular media made countless references to him this being the Messiah that would liberate people from both psychiatry the Knights and the secret use of scientology once the neurosurgeons had finished.
I don't know what happened to him - I think scientology probably rescued him from the gran mals and psychiatrists in the 90's.

He was the dud.

Theres this other guy who is the real deal almost supernaturally.

He seems to have been involved as early as 1978 when the theme tune to Diffrent Strokes says "then along come two they've got nothing but the genes." He seems to have been going strong in the 80's as well when the first episode of Knight Rider mentions the two of them again. "Don't worry about me I'm the original man of steel I've got 10 years on you. It's you I'm worried about still lying on that bed of snakes."

This guy had a gran mal trauma caused by a paedophile maybe just straight after the end of the terrible twos. This meant for all intents and purposes his brain seemed to have stopped developing just on the verge of hatred. And heres the part that even surprised L. Ron his brain started developing again after 5 in the love part of the brain. Effectively meaning he had skipped the hate part of development and went on to develop love. At 9 just before lust develops he had a final gran mal trauma. This meant that he seemed to have a Jesus brain - no hate no lust and full love. His number like the number for Herbie is 7 Of 9 - a Star Trek character.

The best way to describe this guy is with the song from the Lightning Seeds You Showed Me in 1998. This is the same year space shuttle Messiah blasted off in Deep Impact and the fate of the planet was "in the hands of a bunch of retards I wouldn't trust with a potato gun" Armageddon - the same year Will Smith's character shot little Tiffany in the head in Men in Black for reading books too advanced for her age.

It appears according to popular media this guy is still being tortured by psychiatrists and no gran mal diagnosis has been made and everybody is still stuck in their gang. You only need think of the song Symphony by Clean Bandit - if you know about the Assault weapon silence turns into symphonies theres just so many references to him in the popular media.

Katy Perry's ET, many Shakira songs like Eyes Like Yours most of Lady Gaga's songs, Eminem's Cinderella Man, Paul Simon's Pigs Sheep and Wolves describe his dilemma - not being accepted by the gran mals, the scientologists or the Catholic Fraternal Knights which fund psychiatry - a man with no nation.

So thats OT8 truth revealed the scientology movements war with psychiatry and psychiatry's war with scientology is actually "The end of the world as we know it and I feel fine" REM.

Printed in Great Britain
by Amazon

74219799R00020